LOOKING AT HOW ANIMALS LIVE
NIBBLERS AND GNAWERS

K TWINNEY

U.S. text © 1989 by Garrett Educational Corporation
First published in the United States in 1989 by
Garrett Educational Corporation, 130 East 13th Street,
Ada, OK 74820

Original edition published in England under the title of:
LOOKING AT HOW ANIMALS LIVE
NIBBLERS AND GNAWERS

Copyright © 1986 Ilex Publishers Limited

Manufactured in the United States of America

Library of Congress Cataloging in Publication Data

Carwardine, Mark.
  Nibblers and gnawers / written by Mark Carwardine; illustrated by
Dick Twinney.
    p. cm. — (Looking at how animals live)
  "An Ilex book."
  Summary: Discusses a variety of animals who nibble and gnaw with
their teeth, including the chipmunk, flying squirrel, dormouse, and
water vole.
  1. Rodents—Juvenile literature.   [1. Rodents.]   I. Twinney,
Dick, ill.   II. Title.   III. Series: Carwardine, Mark. Looking at
how animals live.
QL737.R6C36   1989
599.32'3—dc20   89-32807
  ISBN 0-944483-29-1   CIP
                                                     AC

LOOKING AT HOW ANIMALS LIVE
NIBBLERS AND GNAWERS

Written by Mark Carwardine
Illustrated by Dick Twinney

An Ilex Book

 **GARRETT EDUCATIONAL CORPORATION**

This series is dedicated to Georgia, aged 7, who
showed us how children look at animals

CONTENTS

Snowshoe hare

Snowshoe, or arctic, hares have special coats to help them survive the winter. As soon as it begins to snow, they change color from brownish gray to pure white. The white coats provide good camouflage, making it harder for foxes, wild cats, golden eagles and other predators to see them against the snowy-white landscape. When the snow begins to melt in the spring, they change back again and their new coats blend in perfectly with the newly colored surroundings.

The white winter coats are much thicker than the summer coats, and the hares fluff them up even more to keep out the cold.

Snowshoe hares live mostly on open, brushy land in Arctic and subarctic regions. They are also found in the Alps and in Ireland.

Although they dig short, simple burrows about six feet long (often in the snow, as well as underground), the adults rarely use them. The burrows are used mostly by young hares — called leverets — to hide from their enemies. These babies can hop within minutes of being born and, like their parents, have very long hind legs for running. Some hares can run at more than fifty miles an hour.

Beaver

In the forested areas of North America and parts of Europe and Asia lives one of the "engineers" of the animal kingdom, the beaver. Rather like a giant rat with a flat tail and webbed hind feet, it is always busy building dams, lodges and canals.

Beavers live in streams and small lakes with trees nearby, in dome-shaped lodges they make out of sticks and mud. These carefully built homes in the water shelter them from bad weather and protect them from enemies such as bears, wolves and coyotes. If a beaver spots danger it slaps its tail onto the water to warn the others, and dives into one of the underwater entrances to the lodge.

Beavers are excellent and graceful swimmers and can stay underwater for as long as fifteen minutes if they have to. Their heavy and waterproof coats help keep them warm, even in icy water, and transparent covers over their eyes act as swimming goggles and help them see underwater.

Beavers work mostly at night, though sometimes they have to begin in the afternoon if they are particularly busy. They fell trees by gnawing the trunks with their teeth. A single beaver can fell an aspen tree in less than half an hour. As the tree begins to

fall, the beaver scampers out of the way and then carefully returns to start cutting it into sections. Each section is dragged or pushed into the water for building.

Beavers don't actually eat the trees, but they do feed on bark, twigs, leaves and roots. They also use the twigs to build a floor inside their lodges.

Capybara

More than four feet long, the capybara is the largest rodent in the world. It looks like a giant guinea pig, which is one of the capybara's closest relatives.

Capybaras are found near ponds, lakes, streams, rivers and swamps in South America. They normally live together in groups of about ten or twenty — though sometimes as many as a hundred may share the same patch of water during the dry season.

They like to spend most of the morning resting and dozing. But during the hottest part of the day they come out to swim or wallow in mud in order to keep cool. They begin to graze in the late afternoon and early evening, using their long teeth to feed on grass that grows in or near the water. They can often be seen standing in water up to their stomachs. During the night, they sleep for short periods but get up regularly to eat more grass.

If capybaras are frightened, they usually run into the water. They sometimes hide in floating vegetation, with their noses sticking up above the surface like snorkels.

DICK TWINNEY

They are excellent swimmers, using their webbed feet like ducks to paddle along, with just their eyes, ears and noses above the surface. They can even hold their breath underwater for five minutes or more.

Baby capybaras are able to walk around and eat grass within a few days of being born. But they get tired very quickly and make easy prey for dogs, foxes, jaguars and other predators.

Chipmunk

Chipmunks can stuff several acorns into their mouths at one time. They often carry them long distances, safely tucked away in cheek pouches, before hiding them under rocks or logs, or inside their burrows.

They spend nearly all their lives collecting food, eating and sleeping. During the summer they are busy every day eating insects and plants. In the autumn, however, they concentrate on gathering nuts and seeds to help them survive the cold winter months.

As winter draws nearer and the weather gets colder, the chipmunks move underground to sleep in their short burrows. Sometimes they stay there for as long as seven months. But at regular intervals they always wake up and eat some of the food they carefully stored the previous autumn.

Closely related to squirrels and marmots, chipmunks are easily identified by the black and white stripes along their backs. They are found in many parts of North America and Asia, where they live mostly in forests and woodlands. Some, however, are also found on mountain slopes and in town parks and gardens.

Flying squirrel

In many woodlands of Asia, northern Europe and North America, strange animals can be seen gliding from tree to tree. They look somewhat like sheets of paper with long tails as they float from the top of one tree to the trunk of the next.

They are flying squirrels. Rather like normal squirrels in appearance, they are just as acrobatic when travelling around in the treetops. But

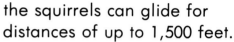

when a branch or a tree is too far away to reach with an ordinary leap, they behave quite differently. They climb as high as they can and then fling themselves into the air. A skin between their arms and legs acts like the wings of a glider. Using their tails for changing direction to avoid branches and other trees,

the squirrels can glide for distances of up to 1,500 feet.

Before taking off, the flying squirrel studies the distance it has to travel very carefully, moving its head from side to side. As it comes in to land, it tilts back slightly, making its ''wings'' turn into a parachute in order to slow down. Then, it immediately runs around to the other side of the tree trunk in case it has been followed by an owl or another predator.

Flying squirrels are most active after dark. They eat food like fruit, nuts, young twigs and tender shoots — but sometimes eat so much that they cannot fly.

Pocket gopher

In some parts of North America, if you are very lucky, you can see whole plants disappearing under the ground. They are being yanked down by pocket gophers, which sometimes nibble at roots entering their underground burrows.

Pocket gophers expertly cut such obstructions as they dig tunnels with their teeth. They never get dirt in their mouths because the teeth stick out through their lips even when their mouths are closed. The only problem is that the teeth grow a fraction of an inch every day — so the gophers constantly have to grind them down by chewing tough food — or by digging new tunnels.

Pocket gophers are not very sociable animals. The only time they live with other pocket gophers is when they have young. For the rest of the year they live alone in their burrows. If two meet accidentally, they often fight to the death.

Their meals are usually quite small but they like to have food available for whenever they feel hungry. So they usually cut it up into small pieces with their teeth, then stuff it into special fur-lined cheek pouches with their paws. Then they empty the pouches into their underground tunnels, to eat whenever they want. It is these pouches, or pockets, which give the gophers their name.

Lemming

There are many stories about lemmings marching to the sea by the thousands and drowning themselves. But they never *try* to get killed — and there are good reasons for taking all the risks involved in their dangerous journeys.

Every three or four years, lemming numbers increase so much that many of the animals are forced out of their homes. When there is not enough space, fights often break out until some decide to leave. Once they are on the move — looking for somewhere else to live — they are so determined that nothing can stop them. But many die from exhaustion or starvation. Some are eaten by predators. Others drown while trying to cross big or dangerous rivers — or by trying to swim across the sea, not realizing how big it is.

Most lemmings live in the coldest, northern parts of the world. But they do not hibernate like other animals. Throughout the

DICK TWINNEY

winter they continue feeding on grasses and sedges as they travel around in tunnels under the snow. It is warmer there than on the surface, where no small animal could survive for long. It is also well protected from enemies such as weasels and foxes.

In the summer, they make similar tunnels and paths through the grass or under roots.

Muskrat

Muskrats spend most of their time in water. In very cold weather, they even swim around and hunt for food underneath the ice. Excellent swimmers and divers, they paddle with their ducklike feet and steer with their tails.

Muskrats live in the marshes, lakes, ponds and streams of North America. They have also been released by people in many parts of Europe and Central Asia, where they are now quite common. They are about the size of small rabbits. Not very agile on land, they can easily be caught by foxes, raccoons and other predators. In water, they expertly swim away from danger and can hold their breath for as long as fifteen minutes if necessary. Baby muskrats can swim when they are only three weeks old.

DICK TWINNEY

Muskrats eat a variety of food. Most of the time they feed on water plants, but sometimes they also catch crabs and shellfish.

Although some muskrats dig tunnels in the banks of streams or lakes, most build beaver-like homes in the water. These are made of water plants, piled into mounds and held together with mud. The muskrats gnaw out tunnels and rooms inside the mounds, where they can keep dry and sleep — safely hidden from alligators.

21

Black rat

Black rats will eat almost anything. They are particularly fond of fruit and peppers, but will also nibble farmers' crops, sugar cane, coconuts and almost anything else they can get their teeth through. This makes them very unpopular. They even gnaw through electrical wires.

Really giant mice, black rats are found in towns and cities throughout the world. They live in warehouses, supermarkets, restaurants, shops, houses and other buildings. In fact, they rarely live away from buildings, except on a few islands in the Caribbean and the Pacific.

DICK TWINNEY

Black rats do not walk around like most other animals. They prefer to run very quickly for a short distance, then stop and stay quite still (to get their breath back and make sure it is safe to continue) before sprinting on again. They are very agile animals and can even climb a vertical piece of wire.

Their greatest enemies, apart from people, are cats. But they are also eaten by snakes, owls, weasels and a variety of other predators.

Dormouse

Dormice are famous for their long winter sleep, which lasts for seven months or more. Curled up, they look like tiny balls of fur, hidden in special nests under leaves or moss, or in a rotten log.

In preparation for this long sleep, dormice begin stuffing themselves with food in the early autumn. They eat as many nuts and seeds and

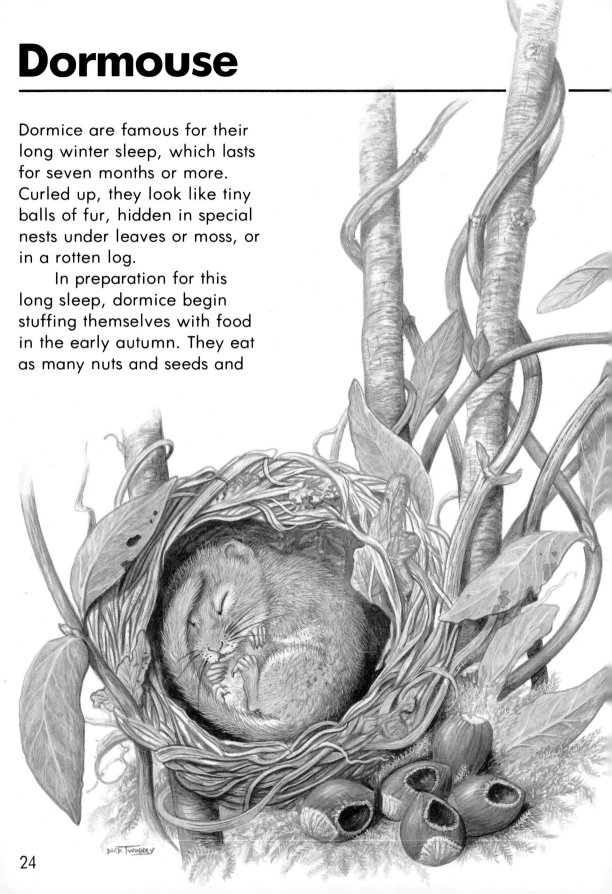

DICK TWINNEY

as much fruit as they can. By the time they are ready for winter they are so fat that they have nearly doubled in weight. During their sleep, or hibernation, they live off this stored fat. By the time they wake up in the spring they are much, much thinner.

The first thing the dormice do on waking is to search for more food. They live mostly in woods, hedgerows and gardens and scramble about in the trees and bushes with great agility.

Different kinds of dormice live in many different parts of Europe, Africa and Asia. Their young are born any time of the year from May onwards, in a nest made of leaves, grass and moss, as well as a few hairs and feathers. There are usually about four young in each litter and they leave the nest when they are between one month and six weeks old. Then they grow really quickly until it is time once again for the dormice to begin hibernating. They disappear inside their nests and see nothing of the outside world until they emerge again the following spring.

Chinchilla

The chinchilla looks like a cross between a rabbit and a squirrel. It is about the same size as both these animals. Found high up in the barren and rugged mountains of the South American Andes, it is most active at dusk, dawn and during the night.

Chinchillas can survive the extremely cold weather of their mountainous homes with the help of their thick, silky soft coats. Their fur is more than an inch thick and helps to keep out the freezing winds.

Unfortunately, people also like to wear chinchilla coats. Their fur is very valuable and many of the animals have been killed to make coats and jackets. As a result, although chinchillas were once common — and it was possible to see thousands of them in a single day — they are now quite rare.

Chinchillas eat mostly plants. They hold bark, grasses, herbs and other food in their forepaws, like a squirrel, while they nibble at it with their long front teeth. Because these teeth never stop growing, chinchillas have to gnaw on hard substances to continually wear them down.

Pika

Every autumn, pikas spend hours on end gathering their winter food supply. They carry mouthfuls of grasses, weeds, mosses and lichens, and pile them up on the ground near their burrows. They even climb into the trees and cut off twigs to add to the collection.

When the pile is several feet high they stop collecting and busy themselves guarding the food from other pikas. They chase away any intruder that tries to steal a twig or a leaf. They are very noisy animals, always barking or bleating at one another. Although they are active throughout the winter, plants are very scarce — so pikas could not survive without their pile of food.

DICK TWINNEY

Pikas usually live in rather remote areas, away from people. They are found in parts of western North America, Asia and south-eastern Europe, where they live on grassy plains, in deserts and on mountain slopes.

Pikas are lively little animals, considerably smaller than their relatives, the rabbits and hares. Most active during the morning and late afternoon, they like to spend the rest of the daylight hours sitting on a rock and peacefully watching the world go by.

Wombat

Wombats are rarely seen in the wild because they are extremely shy animals. They normally come out only at night but sometimes can be found during the day, sunbathing in a shallow resting place next to a tree or log.

Most of the daytime is spent in underground burrows. Wombats dig these themselves with their short, powerful legs and sharp claws. Each burrow may be ninety feet long and have several entrances and different rooms. Wombats are rapid and powerful diggers.

They can even use their teeth, which are very sharp, to cut away roots and other obstructions.

Three feet or more long, they are quite large animals. They look rather like small bears, but their closest relative is the koala. Found in southeast Australia, Tasmania and on some nearby islands, wombats live mostly in eucalyptus forests and, to a lesser extent, coastal grasslands. Unlike koalas, however, they spend all their time on the ground.

A single young wombat is born at almost any time of the year. It spends the first six or seven months of its life in its mother's pouch, which, unlike that of a kangaroo, faces backwards. Gradually, the young animal becomes more independent, but it continues to use the pouch as a base until it is almost a year old.

Volcano rabbit

Within a thirty-minute drive of Mexico City lives the volcano rabbit, one of the rarest rabbits in the world. It is only to be found on the slopes of just two volcanoes in the area.

DICK TWINNEY

Volcano rabbits are the smallest of all rabbits and hares. They also have smaller ears than most other members of their family.

Small groups of up to five usually live together, mostly in the grassy undergrowth of open pine forests. There they live in burrows underground, or beneath suitable piles of rock. Each burrow has many exits for escaping, and a warm nest of grass, dried leaves and rabbit fur.

Volcano rabbits are most active in the daytime and particularly like to sit out in the sun on cold mornings and after heavy rainstorms. They also come out at night and at dusk and dawn.

They have shorter legs than most other rabbits and tend to move in a series of trots rather than by hopping. But they still thump their hind legs on the ground like others in the group, and sometimes squeak and bark when they are alarmed.

Woodchuck

There is a legend in North America that if a woodchuck sees its own shadow on February 2nd, there will be six more weeks of winter. But in the extreme north of their range, which extends from Alaska to Newfoundland, woodchucks sleep during the winter months. It is only in the south, or during spells of particularly mild weather, that woodchucks are out and about in February.

The woodchuck is a marmot, which is a type of squirrel. It feeds mostly on grasses, fruit, grains and vegetables, often sitting up and holding the food in its forepaws to eat.

Woodchucks do not like being with other woodchucks and spend most of the year living alone. The only times they put up with the presence of others is during the breeding season in the spring and, very occasionally, at their favorite feeding sites.

DICK TWINNEY

Woodchucks can see and hear extremely well. This is important because they always have to be on the lookout for bears, coyotes and other enemies. If a female woodchuck feels that her young may be threatened by one of these animals, she often moves them one by one to another nest, carrying them by the scruff of the neck.

Prairie dog

Prairie dogs often stop to kiss and groom one another when they meet. They live in enormous "towns" on the prairies in North America and often visit their neighbors to feed together or to play games.

There are often many thousands of prairie dogs living in one town, in specially built burrows. They put a great deal of time and energy into keeping their homes clean and tidy. In particular, they carefully build up volcano-shaped cones of earth around the burrow entrances, to keep water from running inside when it rains. From a distance, the cones look as if they have been made by giant moles.

Prairie dogs are not dogs but squirrels. The towns therefore attract lots of predators. So when they are not playing, eating grass and seeds, or sunbathing, prairie dogs are busy looking out for danger. As soon as a fox or another predator is seen, a lookout calls to warn the others — and they all rush to hide underground.

When they think the fox has at last disappeared, a few brave individuals peer out cautiously from the safety of their burrows. If they are sure the coast is clear, they signal to the others and, once again, the landscape becomes dotted with prairie dogs.

37

Red squirrel

Red squirrels are always fighting and chasing one another. They race through the trees, biting each other's tails and screaming. If they get really angry, they even stamp their feet.

They usually get up about half an hour before sunrise. But if it is very windy, raining or snowing, they prefer to stay in their nests, or dreys. Eventually, though, they have to come out — even if the bad weather continues — because they cannot survive more than a few days without food.

Red squirrels feed mostly on seeds from pine cones, sometimes while hanging upside down from a branch. Each red squirrel can eat as many as a hundred and fifty cones a day, taking about three minutes to remove and eat all the seeds from each one.

If there is plenty of food about, the squirrels sometimes bury whatever is left. Usually, when they come back to look for it, they remember the general area in which it was hidden but then have to search more closely by smell.

Red squirrels are found in many woods in Europe and parts of Asia. They prefer coniferous forests and can climb trees very quickly, using their tails for balance. But they are often difficult to see because if they feel in danger, they press themselves flat against the bark and stay perfectly still.

Water vole

Water voles are rat-sized, shaggy little animals with water-resistant fur. They live on the plant-covered banks of rivers, ponds and canals, where they eat grass and rushes. Sitting hunchbacked

DICK TWINNEY
86

for hours on end, they simply push the food into their mouths.

Voles are not very good at walking on dry land but are superb swimmers and divers. They are equally at home both on the surface and underwater. They are more often heard than seen, as they "plop" into the water and disappear.

Water voles live in tunnels along riverbanks all over Europe and in many parts of Asia. Very often, the tunnels have holes underwater. These enable the voles to swim straight out of their homes without having to walk on land.

Their tiny young are born underground, at first with no fur and with their eyes closed. But they grow up very quickly and leave the nest when they are only about three weeks old. By that time they are already half the size of their parents.

Many of the youngsters are eaten by giant fish called pike, and by other animals. Even those that escape do not have very long to explore their watery surroundings because water voles only live for about two years.

Golden hamster

Golden hamsters are very popular as pets. They are also common animals in the wild. Found in many parts of Europe and Asia, they live along riverbanks, in fields, in deserts and even on mountain slopes.

Hamsters have enormous pouches in their cheeks. These are used like shopping baskets to carry food. Seeds, shoots and roots are all taken to hamsters' underground burrows, then squeezed out of the pouches with the hamsters' front paws. Their underground homes have special storerooms, as well as a toilet and bedrooms.

Larger items of food, like potatoes, are carried in their front teeth, or literally dragged back to the burrows.

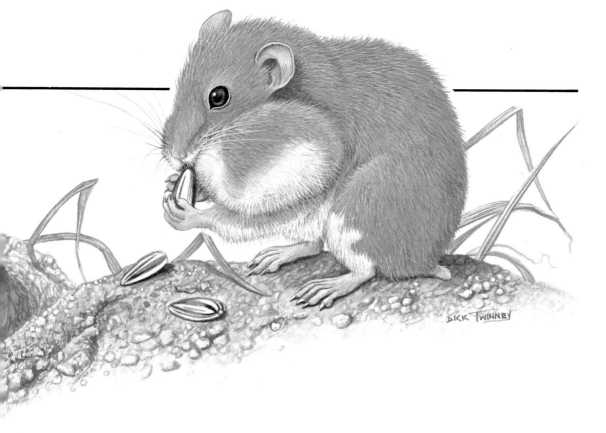

Some people believe that hamsters also use their cheek pouches as "floats" for swimming. When they swim across streams, they blow their pouches up with air to avoid sinking.

Like many other nibblers and gnawers, hamsters spend the winter asleep in their burrows. They wake up on warmer days to eat some of the food from their stores, but do not go outside again until the following spring.

Harvest mouse

The harvest mouse is like a little grassland monkey. It spends a great deal of its time scrambling around in the tops of grass stems and other stiff-stalked vegetation. An excellent climber, it even has a monkey-like tail that can be curled around a stalk and can easily hold the animal's weight.

Harvest mice live in grasslands, hedgerows, reedbeds and bramble patches in many parts of Europe and Asia. Busy at night as well as during the day, they are very active animals, quietly moving around like acrobats in search of insects, seeds, fruits and berries. They always like to test the strength of stems before climbing onto them.

But harvest mice are frightened very easily. They "freeze" if they hear a rustling sound or detect movement, but they can race through the stalks with daring leaps.

In summer, they build breeding nests high above the ground. Made of grass leaves, the nests are about the size and shape of a croquet ball. At first, the entrance hole is kept closed, particularly during the

beginning of the youngsters' lives. As the grass dies back, when winter draws near and the young have left, the mice have to build new nests, this time nearer the ground or in bushes.

Other books in this series

ANIMALS IN THE COLD
ANIMALS ON THE MOVE
MONKEYS AND APES
NIGHT ANIMALS
WATER ANIMALS